Editorial

Dear Reader,

We want to welcome you to our PREMIERE EDITION ONLINE Magazine, Silent Angels Network. The theme is titled "FAITH, HOPE & LOVE". Many years ago, Raymond Smith had a vision, to see people in need helped all over the world. From blankets and water bottles delivered to flooded areas to training materials and books provided to underdeveloped countries, just some of the areas you will read about amongst the website. His Pastor, Evangelist compassionate heart has been relentless in the pursuit to see the Lord glorified in our midst. Pushing through the trials and struggles that presented themselves and yet still, God remains strong. Sanway has expanded its coverage and continues to enlarge its territory to provide materials, encouragement and equipping tools to many. It is from this heart, the donations and contributions of many that thousands have and will receive the blessings of God. When you contribute to SanWay you are partnering and saying "yes" to God.

We have entered a new season, or rather a new era. One that will be remembered for years to come. The Silent Angels Network Magazine has gone LIVE. Your life may be filled with many emotional twists and turns as the world goes through such upheaval. I encourage you to settle in, buckle down and within the pages of this magazine may you find hope, and courage to pursue the things of God. F Agape _____ God's plan for your life. May you experience the presence of God in the midst of the pages as words of life come forth. We are so excited to share this platform with other writers, connections and contributors from other social media platforms.

Let this magazine be unto the Lord to inspire and solidify truth and encouragement when times may not seem so bright. Or maybe you do feel the joy of the Lord and this just adds to your daily devotions. Please take time to share the stories. Be the light in this dark world.

Would you come away with us on this new journey? Let's get to know each other as we share life one story at a time. You are not alone. In closing, Beloved if you are in need of prayer, please fill out the prayer contact card on the website and we will follow up with the Promises of God over your situation. For any information or for article submissions we encourage you to email sanway books

at resmith110435@gmail.com.

As Mother Theresa has said,

Yesterday is gone. Tomorrow has not yet come. We have only today. Let us begin.

Heart to Heart.
God's Richest Blessing.

Diane Nolan
Editor

Silent Angels Network Magazine

Silent Angels Nonprofit was established in 1991, to serve needs across the U.S. and around the world.

In This Issue

Editorial - 1

Four Types of Love - 3

Faith Page - 3

Youth Motivation - 6

What is Hope? - 7

Fasting - 8

How Can a Man Love an Independent Woman - 9

God's Love and Our Obedience to Him - 11

Absolute Truth - 13

Message from David Akuto - 13

History of Silent Angels Network - 17

Mission Funding - 18

4th of July

The 4th of July is an American tradition that has a lot of meaning. To the children, it represents watermelon, ice cream, fun and games, and fireworks. To the adults, although they love the same activities, there is more to celebrate. It is also called Independence Day, the Fourth (4th) of July is a public holiday in the United States of America that commemorates the adoption of the Declaration of Independence on July 4, 1776, which declared the original colonies to be free from British rule.

Silent Angels Magazine Staff

Publisher, Raymond E. Smith
Editor, Diane Nolan
Mission Fund Coordinator, Don Belton
Staff Writers,   Jackson Maina
                 Obed Anthony Oben
Guest Writers,   Roger A. Nutt
                 David Akuto
                 June Lackey
                 Alan Goff

Publisher's Note: The mention of a person in this magazine does not necessarily mean that we endorse them, nor acknowledge their beliefs.

Silent Angels Network Magazine

I am a Silent Angel

I am a Silent Angel, I travel far and wide,
Sometimes those who are destitute still have a lot of pride.

I give blankets to the homeless, and help those who plead,
Sometimes it takes very little to fill their greatest need.

I try to spread seeds of kindness everywhere I go,
Failure to be of service would be my greatest woe.

You can be a Silent Angel by showing others that you care,
Sharing what God has given you with the less fortunate everywhere.

When our life is over and we fall before Jesus on our knee,
He will say, "If you helped your brother, you did it unto me."

- Raymond E. Smith

This poem, along with 80 pages of poems is available in a book titled "Inspirations."
www.sanwaybooks.com.

Four Types of Love

In our English speaking culture we use the word "love" in many ways. We "love" tacos. We "love" our friend's new haircut. We "love" our spouses. Love is a powerful thing. But due to our limited vocabulary we tend to throw it all in one box. So, let's start on an adventure of understanding what the Word says about the different types of love – and in the process – figure out which box our tacos belong in and which our loved ones belong in.

(Continued on page 4)

Faith ... I Will Never Leave Thee

When we walk by Faith HE says "I WILL NEVER LEAVE THEE"

"……. For he has said, I will never leave thee, nor forsake thee" (Hebrews 13:56)

Through the rough road, we believe there is a hand leading, supporting and even carrying or stopping us from stumbling. When we sail on the rough seas, the waves/tides may rise so high attempting to cover us or swallow us up, but we have that conviction and assurance that the master of the seas won't let it get out of control. We walk by faith because we know He is there

We remain still, knowing that He is God and will do what he says.

A few months ago a Christian a couple and their three kids found themselves in what seemed like a hopeless situation, but their conviction and assurance remained steadfast in the Lord.

They had moved into this area to serve the Lord, and then a crisis had erupted. The militias were fighting against the government army. The government decided to stop all gatherings.

This couple who had spent the last months winning souls for Christ and conducting Bible Studies were faced with a great challenge, either to forsake the work or stay and accept the torments. The military paid them a visit one night and promised to shoot down the whole family and burn them up anytime they tried to gather, study the Bible or sing songs. The military accused the couple of assembling criminals in the name of worshiping God. Three days later the militia also visited the couple

(Continued on page 4

Silent Angels Network Magazine

Four Types of Love

(From page 3)

Storge love is the familial love, often referred to as the empathy bond. It is the love found between family members, and those that are bonded together by chance – not choice. An example of this type of love would be the natural love and affection that exists between a parent and a child. Loyalty also falls under storge love and if not tempered with agape love and wisdom, can prove to be unbalanced and become a hindrance in many ways.

What Is Meaning And Definition Of The Four Loves Philia Eros Storge Agape:

Love self is a highly complicated emotion that is almost impossible to understand or explain. Most people tend to believe that love originates from the heart, but it actually starts in the brain. Researchers and psychologists, writers and poets, all have symbolized the heart as the love symbol, but in reality, it is the brain that generates chemical reactions to make one feel loved. There are many different types and kinds of expressing love, and there are many different classifications of love in every culture. The Ancient Greeks symbolize love in four forms, Philia, Eros, Storge, and Agape. All these four types of love enhance a passionate and progressive relationship. Every relationship should have all these four loves existing and working together at the same time to ensure it lasts for a long time.

Philia is love that lies within a friendship or shared goodwill. Philia is the strong bond that exists between people who share the same values, interests, or activities, or even self-love. It is dispassion-

(Continued on page 5)

Faith ... I Will Never Leave Thee

(From page 3)

and threatened to shoot them down if they didn't reveal what they discussed with the military. The couple told the military what the military said and the militia ordered them to stop worshiping or they would be shot down and burnt on their next visit to them. When the militia left, the couple sang, prayed and read the scriptures. All who heard them, named them stubborn, stupid and other names.

The couple believed that God would never leave nor forsake them, and thus kept their faith unwavering.

On Sunday morning as they gathered for worship, the military bashed into the couple's parlor and asked them to stand up. They obeyed. The leader of the military team asked the man why he had continued to disobey their orders. The Christian man replied that they believed in God and had assurance that since they did his will, He would not leave them. The leader asked the man to gather the Bible, songbook and the Communion tray and set them on fire, the Christian man told the leader he could not do, and as the leader of the military team, being a Muslim lifted up his gun to fire at the Christian man and his wife, he found out that his right hand and legs had gone numb. He could not lift up the hand again and fell down, the man shouted and asked his colleagues to carry him out of that place for the Christian were tormenting him. He was carried out of the house, into the military vehicle. He kept shouting that he couldn't see and that his body was on fire.

Two of the other military men returned and

(Continued on page 5)

Silent Angels Network Magazine

(From page 6)

or activities, or even self-love. It is dispassionate, virtuous love. In this case, friendship is described as the non-biological, organic, instinctive, intuitive, gregarious, and necessary. It is the least natural of loves because humans do not need friendship in order to reproduce or regenerate. It is considered to be a higher-level love mainly because it is freely chosen. In earlier civilizations, it was the happiest and is the most full form of love but is often ignored in modern times. It is an intense form of love, though very few can glue its worth because very few can experience true friendship. It is an affectionate, warm, and tender form of platonic or non-romantic love. It ignites a desire to be friends with someone. This is the reason we sometimes feel drawn towards certain people, and we sometimes feel more attached to a friend than our family.

For example, love between friends, acquaintances, associates, groups, etc.

Eros is the sensual or sexual love that arouses romantic feelings, and that drives a romantic relationship. Eros is being in love with someone or loving someone intimately in terms of sexual passion, excluding raw form of sexuality. The main differentiating factor being wanting a lover or wanting one specific mate. It is one of the most desirable forms of all pleasures. It has both a positive and a negative connotation, appealing to both good and evil. It is an intense form of love that often compels to fall in love and have sexual desires for someone. This kind of love exists in the beginning phase of a new relationship, and it may last for too long unless it is taken to the next level. It starts with love with outer beauty, but it can later transform into the love for

From page 4)

asked the Christian man to help them, that they didn't want to suffer the same effect.

He taught them the word of God and they were baptized. They always come to worship with these couple and have built a military post close to the couple's house, they have chased the militia on two occasion who came to attack the couple. When we believe in the Lord, he remains there for us, he confirms his word, fulfill his promises and even though we may not know how He works, we are assured of his promises.

The Bible contains men who remain steadfast despite the persistent trouble/tribulation they went through.

When we consult Hebrews 11:1-11, we find that there is Biblical Hero seemingly have nothing in common. Their unwavering believes.

We need to remain steadfast in our journey of Christianity. We will go through not only seas, tornadoes and even the death of a loved one or even Bankruptcy, but we are assured that he will never leave nor forsake us. Faith is being assured and convinced of the unseen things and hopeful that these things will come to pass as the father has promised. Even in the midst of the Corona Virus or terminal illness, we need to stay focused because the master of the seas will not sleep nor slumber. He knows it all and will do the best for us.

About the Author

Abed Anthony Eben is a preacher who began his work in Kumba, Cameroon. Abed Anthony Eben is a preacher who began his work in Kumba, Cameroon. He is now in Nigeria.

Silent Angels Network Magazine

Silent Angels Needs Members

Silent Angels Nonprofit has been in existence for the past 30 years. We have served people with needs throughout the USA and some foreign countries. We depend on members to help us to carry on with this great work. We one joins Silent Angels, they receive a beautiful certificate like the one below.

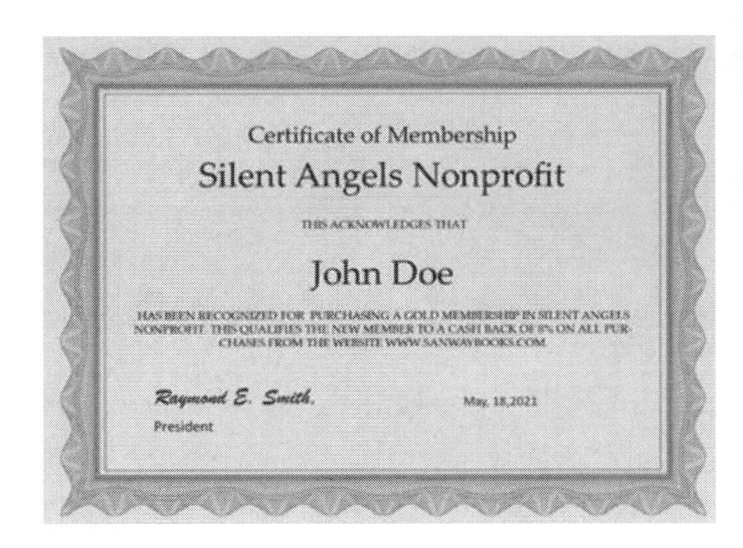

Four Types of Love

(From page 5)

ate, virtuous love. In this case, friendship is described as the non-biological, organic, instinctive, intuitive, gregarious, and necessary. It is the least natural of loves because humans do not need friendship in order to reproduce or regenerate. It is considered to be a higher-level love mainly because it is freely chosen. In earlier civilizations, it was the happiest and is the most full form of love but is often ignored in modern times. It is an intense form of love, though very few can glue its worth because very few can experience true friendship. It is an affectionate, warm, and tender form of platonic or non-romantic love. It ignites a desire to be friends with someone. This is the reason we sometimes feel drawn towards certain people, and we sometimes feel more attached to a friend than our family. For example, love between friends, acquaintances,

> So now faith, hope, and love abide, these three; but the greatest of these is love. 1 Corinthians 13:13

associates, groups, etc.

Youth Motivation

Two years ago, Kitalibara Joseph, who lives in Kasese, Uganda, and I discussed how he could start teaching classes to the youth in his area. The idea sounded good to me, since I had written a book on Motivation. As usual, I like to check out the people with whom I work. I talked with someone who have been working in Uganda for some time. He gave high regards about Joseph and his wife Ruth.

I sent Joseph the book I wrote on Success and Motivation. I followed up with copies by email for the students to use as a study guide. Joseph also taught classes on skills; carpentry, welding, masonry, sewing, driving, etc.

The first class was successful. I got message from some of the students saying how much they liked the classes. The student were being taught that they do not have to remain in their present circumstances, they can rise above and improve their lives.

(Continued on page 9)

What is Hope?

Let's start by taking a look at what hope is from both a dictionary definition and a biblical one.

Hope (Dictionary)

The general consensus from all dictionary definitions is that hope is a feeling of expectation, a desire or wish for a certain thing to happen.

Hope (Bible)

A biblical definition of hope takes it one step further. Hope is an expectation with certainty that God will do what he has said. I hope you can see the difference. One is a wish or desire, the other is a certainty or guarantee.

Let me use a verse from Scripture to illustrate the point.

"Now faith is confidence in what we hope for and assurance about what we do not see" (Hebrews 11:1).

Why do I bring up this verse? You cannot have hope unless it is tied together with faith. In essence, you have hope because you have faith and you have faith because you have hope. However, you don't just have faith in faith or hope in hope, there is no real value in that. What matters most is the object of your faith and hope – that makes all the difference.

The thing that separates the basic definition of hope and the biblical definition of hope is what I call The God Factor. Your hope should be based on the fact of who God is and nothing else. If God is not the object of your hope then you don't have true biblical hope because the certainty has been removed. Without that, your hope simply reverts back to a wish.

Why Can You Have Hope?

There is one underlying reason why hope should spring into your heart as a believer. God cannot lie. Consider this scripture in Hebrews:

"Because God wanted to make the unchanging nature of his purpose very clear to the heirs of what was promised, he confirmed it with an oath. God did this so that, by two unchangeable things in which it is impossible for God to lie, we who have fled to take hold of the hope set before us may be greatly encouraged. We have this hope as an anchor for the soul, firm and secure" (Hebrew 6:17-19, emphasis added).

If God has said it, you can trust his promise because it is impossible for God to lie. This trust therefore becomes an anchor for the soul. Anchors are designed to keep you steady so that you will not be moved. This anchor that it is impossible for God to lie is the foundation for your certainty and the backbone for your hope. It is the reason why you can have hope today.

I call this type of hope "in spite of." In spite of what you see; in spite of what is going on; in spite of how dire the situation looks; you can have hope because God cannot lie. Regardless of your situation, find out what God has said about it and let that be the truth you believe about it. This does not guarantee that your situation will change immediately but the beauty of hope is that even if the situation remains, so does your hope. Because of hope you have confidence knowing God will respond and come through on your behalf. If that is what he said you can be certain that is what he will do.

(Continued on page 10)

Is Fasting a Requirement for Christians Today

Several days ago I posted this question on Facebook, and got 65 comments. Many comments were just a Yes or No. Some gave a detailed answer. Should you have ever considered this question, you may find your answers here.

Even though fasting for a Christian is not a requirement, it is a necessity. The Bible highly encourages Christians to fast from food and water for a period of time. Biblical Fasting in Today's Church. Although fasting is not required, it is highly encouraged by Christ, Himself.

Christians today would do well to consider fasting as a means of drawing closer to God, or gaining spiritual strength. It is not a command; it is a privilege. In times of great stress it is a way of communicating with the Lord, and if it is sincere and dedicated to God, it will be regarded by him.

Christians are not required to fast. However, it's highly recommended to fast as a believer, and Jesus Himself expects it of us. This is to be more spiritually fed and more intimate in a relationship with the Lord.

Fasting, in the biblical sense, is the abstaining from food and drink for a spiritual reason.

In the Old Testament era, the Jews fasted frequently, though there was only one fast prescribed by the law. Once each year on the Day of Atonement the Hebrews were to afflict their souls (Lev. 16:31), which meant fasting (cf. Isa. 58:3).

When the Lord's disciples were criticized for not fasting, Jesus responded by suggesting that it was hardly appropriate for them to fast while he was yet with them. The time would come, however, when he would be taken away from them. Then they would fast (Lk. 5:35).

The reason why fasting is not required is that there's not one place written in the Bible to demand believers to fast. Also, in all thirteen letters apostle, Paul writes, there is not one piece of the works of literature mention a command of fasting. When you fast, do not look somber as the hypocrites do, for they disfigure their faces to show others they are fasting. Truly I tell you, they have received their reward in full. Matthew 6:16

NOTE: To know the truth about any requirements or beliefs, I recommend that you go to the source, the Bible. "Ye shall know the truth and the truth will set you free."

- Raymond E. Smith

Please send questions or comments

Urgent Request

Jackson Maina is in need of a computer or a laptop. He is a Gospel Preacher and serves on our writing staff. Should anyone have a device to assist him to do his work, contact him by email: jitati59@gmail.com.

Youth Motivation

(From page 6)

Joseph was contacted by the officials, who warned him that he would have to register the classes with the government. There was no money to pay the registration fee. Classes were suspended until the money could be raised. Meanwhile, Joseph has paid part of the fee from money he earned.

The same students, as well as others are begging for more classes. They realized the usefulness of the class and how that they could help others as well as help themselves. Joseph needs $500.00 to continue these valuable classes. Your donations will be very much appreciated.

Donations for Youth Motivation may be made by sending to paypal, resmith110435@gmail.com.

"We are debtors to every man to give him the Gospel in the same measure in which we have received it." — P.F. Bresee

---

How Does a Man Love an Independent Woman

Alan Goff - The Alan Goff Community

Men in a relationship with an independent woman often find it a challenge to know how to connect with, support and love her in a way that strengthens the bond.

We struggle with our masculine energy, male instinct, and ego that tells us we need to be the hunter, provider, protector and leader. Our confidence and sense of security is tied into feeling needed.

So how can a man love an independent woman and still feel like a man?

By no longer accepting what he's been programmed to believe about male and female roles. By seeing her as his equal partner in life. By admiring her strength and courage and giving her the respect, acceptance and trust she's earned and deserves.

She has fought hard to stand up for herself and her right to live the life she wants - how she wants. A way of life that gives her the freedom to be herself and do what makes her happy. She doesn't want to be told what to do, how to feel or need permission from anyone. She is free - and if you really love her, you will support her so she always feels that way.

The easier you make it for her to love, respect and value herself, the more she will love, respect and value you. The more you show you trust her, the more she will want to reward that trust.

A loving relationship is not based on dependency, control or insecurity, it's built upon mutual love, trust and respect. A strong woman wants to be with a strong man, a man who doesn't live in fear. Confidence is sexy; jealousy, insecurity and neediness are not.

If you want to love an independent woman, you need to be an independent man. A man who is not afraid of being vulnerable with his feelings, yet confident enough to let her come to him when she wants him.

If you stop trying to make her need you, she will show you how much she wants you.

About The Author

Alan Goff is an experienced platform speaker who inspires, motivates and moves you to action. When he steps up to the podium, Alan multiplies value to your meeting, special event or conference.

Alan is the President of Achieving Goals Incorporated, a principle-based process training and consultancy company that equips & motivates individuals and organizations to improve significantly from the inside out. Their mission is to develop people and build business.

Silent Angels Network Magazine

(From page 10)

Promises to Give You Hope

The verses I am going to share with you are all things God has said he will do for you. (By the way there are more, I just couldn't fit them all in one article.) As you read these remember what hope is, knowing that God will come through for you.

The hope of God's provision

"So do not worry, saying, 'What shall we eat?' or 'What shall we drink?' or 'What shall we wear?' For the pagans run after all these things, and your heavenly Father knows that you need them" (Mathew 6:31-32).

"And my God will meet all your needs according to the riches of his glory in Christ Jesus" (Philippians: 4:19).

The hope of God's presence

"Be strong and courageous. Do not be afraid or terrified because of them, for the Lord your God goes with you; he will never leave you nor forsake you" (Deuteronomy 31:6).

The hope of God's protection

"You are my refuge and my shield; I have put my hope in your word" (Psalm119:114).

"For in the day of trouble he will keep me safe in his dwelling; he will hide me in the shelter of his sacred tent and set me high upon a rock" (Psalm27:1,5, 5).

The hope of eternal life

"Paul, a servant of God and an apostle of Jesus Christ to further the Faith of God's elect and their knowledge of the truth that leads to godliness — in the hope of eternal life, which God, who does not lie, promised before the beginning of time" (Titus1:1-2).

The hope of Christ's return

"For the grace of God has appeared that offers salvation to all people. It teaches us to say 'No' to ungodliness and worldly passions, and to live self-controlled, upright and godly lives in this present age, while we wait for the blessed hope—the appearing of the glory of our great God and Savior, Jesus Christ" (Titus2:11-13).

The hope of inheritance

"Praise be to the God and Father of our Lord Jesus Christ! In his great mercy he has given us new birth into a living hope through the resurrection of Jesus Christ from the dead, and into an inheritance that can never perish, spoil or fade. This inheritance is kept in heaven for you" (1 Peter 1:3-4).

The hope of answered prayer

"This is the confidence we have in approaching God: that if we ask anything according to his will, he hears us. And if we know that he hears us—whatever we ask—we know that we have what we asked of him" (1 John5:14-15).

As you can see throughout all these promises The God Factor is woven through them. That is the basis for your hope and the only reason you can have confidence.

Why Is Hope So Important in the Christian Life?

Having a better understanding of what hope is leads to another question. Why is it so important? Here is the answer – hope is what moti-

(Continued on page 12)

God's Love and Our Obedience to Him

In 1John 4:7-11, we have a very powerful lesson. "We know God through love."

In verse 9, we are reminded that "God sent His Son into the world, that we might live through Him." Nothing is more important than loving God and doing his will.

If God loves us we should also love one another. Frequently, it is hard to love others when they disappoint us or act ungodly. But we still need to set the right example.

In 1John 4:12-16, we know that "we see God through love." Verse 16 tells us, "God is love." Just look outside at what God has made: the beauty that surrounds us! The incredible attention to details is far beyond our scope of understanding.

In 1 John 4:17-19, we are reminded of the "consummation of love." It is the final, ultimate love. God's son who died for us is the ultimate gift of love. We can never love like God loves us. We aren't capable of that intensity.

In 1John 4:20-21, we learn "Obedience by faith." In order to please God we have to obey Him. When we obey God, we glorify him with our actions.

Rom.16:25-27, tells us that faith produces obedience and that's the ultimate goal. We gain faith from the Gospel. When we read and study the Bible we grow in faith. We also gain faith from attending worship and Bible class every time the doors are open.

In Rom.5:1, we are told that "We are justified by faith." Our faith and obedience determines our future. It determines whether we hear God say to us " Well done good and faithful servant, enter in" or "Depart from me, I never knew you." Matt.: 21-23.

About The Author

June Lackey

I was born and raised in Key West, FL. I have lived in Jacksonville FL for many years but Key West will always be home. I work in a bookstore with 4 million books. I am in charge of the little kids department. Three grown sons and two grandsons keep me busy. I love, writing children's books and doing genealogy.

Children's E-Books

Daniel was a servant of God. He prayed three times a day. The king made a rule that if anyone prayer to God they would be punished. Daniel continued his prayers daily.

The story of Stone Soup has been told many times, but never like the way we tell it. Although, this story is not from the Bible, it does teach Biblical principle.

These books and many others are available on the website,

www.sanwaybooks.com

Silent Angels Network Magazine

(From page 10)

vates you as a believer. Can you imagine if we had no hope? Paul himself said:

"If only for this life we have hope in Christ, we are of all people most to be pitied" (1 Corinthians 15:19).

Your entire walk as a believer is based on hope. A hope that goes beyond this life and extends throughout eternity. Everything you do as a Christian flow from this. Why do you pray? Hope. Why do you witness? Hope. Why do you endure hardship, trials, or persecution? Hope. Why did many who have gone before us sacrifice, give, serve, even lose their lives for the message of the gospel? One word, hope.

If you remove the element of hope then you will discover that your joy, your enthusiasm, your peace, your focus, your motivation, everything attached to your walk with God will be removed with it. That is why you cannot lose hope. It is also why one of the weapons of Satan is to attack your hope. Think of all the words that are the opposite of hope. Fear, despair, doubt, uncertainty. None of these words inspire and none of these words bring the joy and peace that hope in God brings. That's why you must fight for it at all costs.

But you have help in God. Know today that God is the God of hope, Christ is the hope of Glory and the Holy Spirit is the one who births hope in you. Consider these verses.

"May the God of hope fill you with all joy and peace as you trust in him, so that you may overflow with hope by the power of the Holy Spirit" (Romans 15:13).

"To them God has chosen to make known among the Gentiles the glorious riches of this mystery, which is Christ in you, the hope of glory" (Colossians 1:27).

God does not want you to lose hope today and you don't have to. Keep your trust in the one who is faithful because he will not let you down.

A Prayer for Hope

Lord help me today and this whole month to put my complete hope and trust in you. You are God who cannot lie so if you said it, it will happen. Help me to never lose hope knowing that you will come through and fulfill what you have promised on my behalf.

In Jesus' Name, Amen

What is hope? In one word, everything. God wants to restore your hope today and this month. Hope in him. Hope in his promises. Hope in his word. I don't know your situation today but God does. You can look to him today with confidence and assurance knowing that he will help you in your time of need.

You can put your full hope in that.

"Let us then approach God's throne of grace with confidence, so that we may receive mercy and find grace to help us in our time of need" (Hebrews 4:16).

Let all God's people say amen.

> *Learn about the most unique way of helping to support missions, and give them hope.*
>
> *See page 16*

About The Author

Jackson Maina is from Nairobi, Kenya. He is a gospel Preacher and a staff writer for this magazine. He is the author of "Violence Against Men."

A Message From David Akuto

Greetings, Fellow Christians: I hope this message finds you well, and that you've had a relaxing and blessed week.

Because you are an important part of our cause, I thought you would like to know our big plans. Our congregation is growing, just like any other family, the more members we have the more room we need. We are pleased to invite you to be an important part of this exciting process. This year, we are having plans to raise funds for the purchase of the land. How blessed are we to have so many members like yourself that we need to help us raise support for the Land purchase for our ministry. It is our greatest hope that you'll be able to join us by visiting the website, www.sanwaybooks.com and of course a willing contribution of any size are always accepted.

Rivers do not drink their own water; trees do not eat their own fruits; the Sun does not shine on itself and flowers do not spread fragrance for themselves. Living for others is a rule of nature . We are all born to help each other. No matter how difficult it is, life is good when you are happy. But much better when other are happy because of you. " If you have any question about this cause please feel free to contact our Special Projects Coordinator, brother Don Belton his email is (DBelton0009@protonmail.com). As always have a blessed day. We hope to hear from you.

With Christian love,

David Ochieng Akuto

Absolute Truth

About 15 years ago, a good friend and I decided we needed to teach a middle school age Bible study class on "Absolute Truth". One of the main premises was just because you believe something, doesn't make it true. One of the first examples was about the statement "The God that I know wouldn't (insert belief here)". The class mainly focused on spiritual matters and religion - and we didn't have many real world struggles with "what really is truth?". Now 15 years later, our kids have to try to navigate through a maze of "if you say it" or "if you identify as it" it's true and cannot be questioned. If you dare question the "truthfulness" you will lose your job, your friends and even your family. Parents, please teach your kids and grandkids that there is Truth. The Word of God is Truth. And teach them that standing by the Truth is always right, no matter the consequence.

About the Author

Roger A. Nutt is a member of the West Spartanburg Church of Christ, in Spartanburg, SC. He also serves as a member of State Representative - House District 34, in South Carolina.

Silent Angels Network Magazine

SanWay Book Store

SanWay Book Store carries a large selection of books for both adult and children. Our children's e-books are top of the line for teaching children Bible stores. See the full list by logging onto: www.sanwaybooks.com.

Violence Against Men

This book was thoroughly researched before writing. You will be amazed at what is going on between woman and man. Most cases are not normally revealed. Get the facts in the e-book.

Go to www.sanwaybooks.com. Place your order there. The price is $2.99. It will come to you by e-mail. You car read the book from a computer, laptop, iPad, cell phone, etc. No special device such as a Kindle is necessary.

Written by Jackson Maina

www.sanwaybooks.com

This book is available in English and Swahili.

Order it today

Jackson's second book is being printed.

Children's E-books

Billy Goes to Camp

Raymond E. Smith

Children's E-Books Completed

- The Story of Ruth
- Walking on Water
- David and Goliath
- The Tower of Babel
- Breakfast with Jesus
- Nehemiah the Builder
- Joseph and his Dreams
- Joshua, the Battle of Jericho
- Book of Esther part 1
- Book of Esther part 2
- Book of Esther part 3

These E-Books may be read from a computer, cell phone, iPad, any device where you receive emails. Nothing special needed. Great for birthdays, Christmas and everyday reading. They teach great Bible lessons. Price: $2.99 per each.

Order from: www.sanwaybooks.com

www.sanwaybooks.com

Silent Angels Network Magazine

SanWay General Store

The SanWay General Store is a subsidiary of Silent Angels Network. We sell books, and healthcare products. We are constantly adding more items from which you can choose.

Our books include paperback and e-books. There are 30 e-books for children. You don't need a special device such as a Kindle to read these books. The books are read from you cell phone, computer or iPad.

Some of the books will be displayed in this magazine for you to see.

To view all the books, log onto our website; www.sanwaybooks.com. The sale of these books will help to raise funds for our missions.

Our members also receive a share of the earnings

For Good Health & Well Being

Visit out web page
www.sanwaybooks.com/vitaguard-1

Here are 12 benefits of Ginkgo Biloba.

- Age-related macular degeneration.
- Alzheimer's disease.
- Anxiety.
- Asthma.
- Bronchitis.
- Depression.
- Erectile dysfunction.
- Fatigue.

CBD oil has been studied for its potential role in easing symptoms of many common health issues, including anxiety, depression, acne and heart disease. For those with cancer, it may even provide a natural alternative for pain and symptom relief.

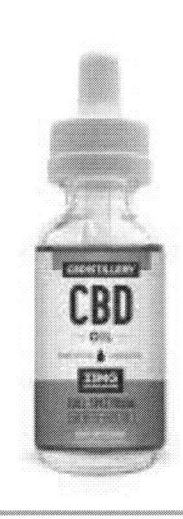

Visit the General Stores for these and many other Healthcare products.

www.sanwaybooks.com

Silent Angels Network Magazine

History of Silent Angels

Silent Angels began in 1991, for the purpose of providing blankets for the homeless. Shortly after the beginning more needs presented themselves and the Silent Angel Network expanded helping in additional ways. Food, household furnishings, medicine, clothing and other needs coast to coast in the U.S. and other parts of the world were provided.

In the past 30 years these are the ways in which Silent Angels Network provided for needs in our world.

Raymond E. Smith. Founder, Silent Angels Network

Smith is a Minister, Author, Key note Speaker, Motivational trainer. In the past he has served as a part-time Minister of the Gospel of four congregations, a Deacon and a Bible class teacher. He has written more than 250 paperback and e-books.

- Blankets for homeless and disaster victims.
- Provided household furnishings too victims of a fire & others.
- Provided medicine and other health needs.
- Donated medical supplies to St. Luke's Free Hospital.
- Bought firefighter's equipment.
- Provided funds for Asian storm victims.
- Assisted Gospel Partners (mission work in India)
- Assisted Southeastern Children's Home.
- Organized "Youth Motivation" a mission (Uganda).
- Assisted with the rebuilding of New Orleans in 2006.
- Provided bottled water after hurricanes and tornados.
- Built an orphan's home in Zambia, 2009.

A New Day Is Dawning

Because of the difficulties of raising funds for mission work, the staff of Silent Angels Network have created a new way to help missions to raise their own funds, along with a staff from Silent Angels Network assisting them.

The following pages will describe the plan of action. We invite our readers to help us in this effort. This plan will allow local evangelist in foreign fields to spend more time with the work for which God has called them.

Please log onto www.sanwaybooks and see more of what of what Silent Angels Network is doing.

Silent Angels Network Magazine

Become a Member of Silent Angels Network
Help Change the Way Funds Are Raised For Missions

Raising funds for mission work is becoming more and more difficult. We receive emails, and messages on Facebook begging for money. There are many reasons why request don't get results.

- One reason is the pandemic. Certainly, the pandemic has put pressure on mission work. Travel restrictions has limited the ability of missionaries to get to the areas in which they normally work. Thus, the people in those areas are not getting some of the provisions they normally receive.

- Some people in areas such as the U.S. are saying, "I would rather use my money to help local people." What would have happened to the rest of the world if the church in Antioch had taken this position? Paul, Barnabas, John, Mark, and their companions would never preached to the rest of the world. Paul would have never made three mission trips, plus his voyage to Jerusalem.

- Another cause for a lack of mission funds is again the pandemic. Church attendance has been down because of mandatory restrictions. Christians have stayed at home. As a result, contributions are being cut back. Some churches have a way to make your contributions online. Not all are doing that.

- There are many factors that can get in the way of making supporting missions a church priority.

- Minister crises

- Marriages on the brink of divorce

- Budgetary shortcomings

- Politics between groups in the church

- Basic human exhaustion from overwork

- As church leaders route energy to other needs, it is extremely common to see missions giving drop at our churches. It's just a reality. But it doesn't have to be that way.

- People give to missions for very specific reasons, and they *stop* giving to missions for specific reasons. Here's how you can spot problems and fix them before they make a long-term impact on your missions program.

A New Approach to Funding Missions

Recognizing that these problems exist, the officials of Silent Angels Network have created an alternative to providing funds for mission work. The founder of Silent Angels Network, has proven that this method works well in business, and his thoughts were, why not use this plan for raising mission fun ding. On the following pages of this magazine you will find how this plan works in full detail. We urge you to read these pages and consider this fundraising method for the missions that you choose.

The Best Plan Ever To Raise Funds For Missions

Membership Plan

Membership	Fee	Mission	Sponsor	Expense	Bonus
Basic	$10.00	$5.00	$2.50	$2.00	$0.50
Bronze	25.00	12.50	6.25	4.00	2.25
Silver	50.00	25.00	12.50	8.00	4.50
Gold	100.00	50.00	25.00	15.00	10.00
Platinum	200.00	100.00	50.00	30.00	20.00

Fee: This is the fee that the new member pays for their membership.

Mission: This is the amount that the mission receives from the new member.

Sponsor: This is the amount the sponsor earns.

Bonus: The bonuses to go into the co-op account.

- Every time a membership is sold the bonus money is placed in the especial account. The members will share in the account, based on their sales.
- Checks are not written until a member has at least $32.00 in their account.
- Bonuses will be paid through PayPal. If you are due a check, and do not have a PayPal account, the fee will be send to you by Western Union and fees will be deducted.
- Once you get a check, your bonus account continues to the next level and you get another check. This continues perpetually.
- As an extra, When a product is sold in the General store, 10% of the sale will be added to the bonus account. This include all books.

To enroll go to the Membership Page   www.sanwaybooks.com

Raising Funds For Mission Work

Our Lord gave us a ministry to seek the lost. Mission work requires a lot of finances. At times we need to do projects of compassion, benevolence and support to help the needs of those in the community.

To do these, we need donors, who are sometimes reluctant because of uncertainty. It is in this angle that Silent angels has developed a way out to help raise funds for mission. It requires purchasing a membership plan. The plans go from basic, bronze, silver, gold and platinum.

When you purchase a membership, the greatest part of the money goes for mission projects, you get a percentage back and the rest stays and grows. I recently acquired a gold membership and these are the benefits: - I am sure of a steady supply of funds for missions in the future. -It will motivate sponsors to see that I am committed to the course. - I have sowed a seed that will eventually become a forest and sustain vast mission efforts.

It is essential for all our missions and missionaries to purchase a membership so as to ensure continuity of their mission work. I encourage to start even from the basic package and grow. It is the best thing to do.

- Abed Anthony Eben

The Theme for the August Issue is "My Life as a Missionary."

Personal Testimony

When the COVID-19 Pandemic started in March of 2020, I started taking Colloidal Silver. I had no idea where the virus was going or how long it would last. I read the benefits and how it could help any type of virus. At that time SanWay became a distributor for the Colloidal Silver and we sold to many customers.

I heard all the negative news about the vaccine and the problems that some people were having as a result of the shot. Frankly, I was afraid to take the vaccine. I increased the dosage of Colloidal Silver about six months ago when the cases of the virus was surging. During the past 15 months, I have not had any kind of virus, flu, or even a cold. I am not making any claims of what the Colloidal Silver will do for you. I can only say what It has done for me.

Don't you think it is worth investigating? Raymond E. Smith

Log onto our website: www.sanwaybooks.com, click on General Store.

When you purchase any healthcare products from our General store, 10% is given to help Missions.

Silent Angels Network Magazine

Suggested uses: Acne, Aids, Allergies, Appendicitis, Arthritis, Athletes Foot, Bladder Infection, Boils, Burns, Cancer, Chronic Fatigue, Cystitis, Dandruff, Diabetes, Eczema, Hay Fever, Hepatis, Leukemia, Pneumonia, Prostate Infections, Ring Worm, Scarlet Fever, Shingles, Viruses, Warts, Yeast Infections, Ear Infections *

*These statements have not been evaluated by the FDA. This product is not intended to diagnose, cure, treat, or prevent any disease.

To order go to website
www.SanWayBooks.com

Vita-Guard Colloidal Silver

"Natural Mineral to Protect From Viruses"

A Natural Dietary Supplement

This high voltage method produces the smallest silver particles without the presence of ions. The critical factors that make a "good" colloidal silver product are particle size, purity and concentration.

60ppm

8 Fl. Ounces

Suggested Use

Take a Teaspoon full morning and evening. Mix with 4 oz. pure water.*

Colloidal Silver is produced with triple steam distilled water with 99.998 pharmaceutical grade silver.

Colloidal Silver can be taken as a dietary supplement to enhance the immune system. Refrigeration not recommended.

Do not take more than directed. An over-dose may turn skin gray.

* These statements have not been evaluated by the FDA. This product is not intended to diagnose, cure, treat, or prevent any disease.

What is Colloidal Silver?

Colloidal silver is a specially made formulation that takes tiny particles of silver and suspends them in water. Commercially available doses of colloidal silver come in both oral and topical forms of this essential mineral. The purity of colloidal silver's ingredients, whether it's topical or oral colloidal silver, should be clearly listed on the bottle or spray to ensure quality. It's an ancient remedy that was once used to treat bacterial, viral and fungal infections.

What is Colloidal Silver used for?

- Oral colloidal silver is most commonly used for: Boosting the immune system.
- Providing a defense against common cold and flu.

Topical colloidal silver is most commonly used for:

- Promoting faster healing of cuts, burns and blisters
- Offering relief for insect bites and stings, rashes, razor burns, sunburns and other skin issues
- Supporting our immune system daily is one of the best ways to confront environmental and dietary challenges and the emotional stressors that weaken our immune system.
- Many people talk about *colloidal silver* not only promoting *hair* growth but also relieving the scalp of dandruff. People have also mentioned a really *health* shine.
- According to New York–based dermatologist Gervaise Gerstner, MD, not only is colloidal silver a great antibacterial, but it has some impressive anti-inflammatory benefits as well, making it an excellent agent for the treatment for hormonal and inflammatory acne, as well as rosacea and inflamed skin.

We have reduced our price to make it affordable to everyone.

Log onto our website:
www.sanwaybooks.com

Silent Angels Network Magazine

When You Enroll in Silent Angels Network
You Will Receive A Certificate Like The One Below.

Certificate of Membership
Silent Angels Nonprofit

THIS ACKNOWLEDGES THAT

John Doe

HAS BEEN RECOGNIZED FOR PURCHASING A GOLD MEMBERSHIP IN SILENT ANGELS NONPROFIT. THIS QUALIFIES THE NEW MEMBER TO A CASH BACK OF 8% ON ALL PURCHASES FROM THE WEBSITE WWW.SANWAYBOOKS.COM.

Raymond E. Smith. May, 18, 2021
President

Your Obligation as a Member

- Simply tell your family and friends about Silent Angels Network.
- Pray for the success and our mission work, and ask God's guidance.
- You may obtain a few magazines like this one and give to key individuals.
- Invite your friends to visit the website: www.sanwaybooks.com

Appreciation

I want to express my appreciation to all the staff of Silent Angels Network, for their diligence, and dedication in publishing the first issue of this magazine. And, thanks to our new members of Silent Angels Network.

- Raymond E. Smith

Silent Angels Network Magazine

Book Publishing

Become an Author

Yes, you can become an e-book Author very quickly and easily. Do you have a story you want to tell? Publish it with SanWay e-book. You no longer need a Kindle or some other E-reader. You can download the e-book onto your computer, laptop, phone, or other devices.

The cost to publish your e-book is only $39.00 (up to 75 pages). For 75-200 pages $49.00   This DOES NOT include editing. We print what you send us. If we edit your book there is an additional cost of $69.00.

How to proceed. Type your e-book in Microsoft Word, or compatible app.
We do the rest! Your book will be published and promoted by SanWay Books.
Send your manuscript to resmith110435@gmail.com.

Questions & Answers

Question: How much do I earn as an author?
Answer: We pay you 35% of the selling price.

Question: How do I price my book?
Answer: The minimum price of an e-book is $2.99. It depends on the content of the book and the value to those who will read it.

Question: Do I pay for advertising?
Answer: No. We do the advertising on SanWay's website and magazine. You can increase your sales by promoting it on social media such as Facebook and Twitter.

Silent Angels Network Magazine

A Prayer

Now I sit me down in school
   Where praying is against the rule
For this great nation under God
   Finds mention of Him very odd.
If scripture now the class recites,
   It violates the Bill of Rights.
And anytime my head I bow
   Becomes a Federal matter now.
Our hair can be purple, orange or green,
   That's no offense; it's a freedom scene..
The law is specific, the law is precise.
   Prayers spoken aloud are a serious vice.
For praying in a public hall
   Might offend someone with no faith at all..
In silence alone we must meditate,
   God's name is prohibited by the State..
We're allowed to cuss and dress like freaks,
   And pierce our noses, tongues and cheeks...
They've outlawed guns, but FIRST the Bible.
   To quote the Good Book makes me liable.
We can elect a pregnant Senior Queen,
   And the 'unwed daddy,' our Senior King.
It's 'inappropriate' to teach right from wrong,
   We're taught that such 'judgments' do not belong..
We can get our condoms and birth controls,
   Study witchcraft, vampires and totem poles...
But the Ten Commandments are not allowed,
   No word of God must reach this crowd.
It's scary here I must confess,
   When chaos reigns the school's a mess.
So, Lord, this silent plea I make:
   Should I be shot; My soul please take!
Amen

Copied from Facebook. Written by a 12 year old boy. He got an A+ for his work.

Blessings For Helping The Poor

Psalms 41:1-3

Blessed is he that considereth the poor: the LORD will deliver him in time of trouble.

² The LORD will preserve him, and keep him alive; and he shall be blessed upon the earth: and thou wilt not deliver him unto the will of his enemies.

³ The LORD will strengthen him upon the bed of languishing: thou wilt make all his bed in his sickness.

Proverbs 28:7

The righteous care about justice for the poor, but the wicked have no such concern.

Proverbs 3:27-28

Do not withhold good from those to whom it is due, when it is in your power to act. Do not say to your neighbor, "Come back tomorrow and I'll give it to you"—when you already have it with you.

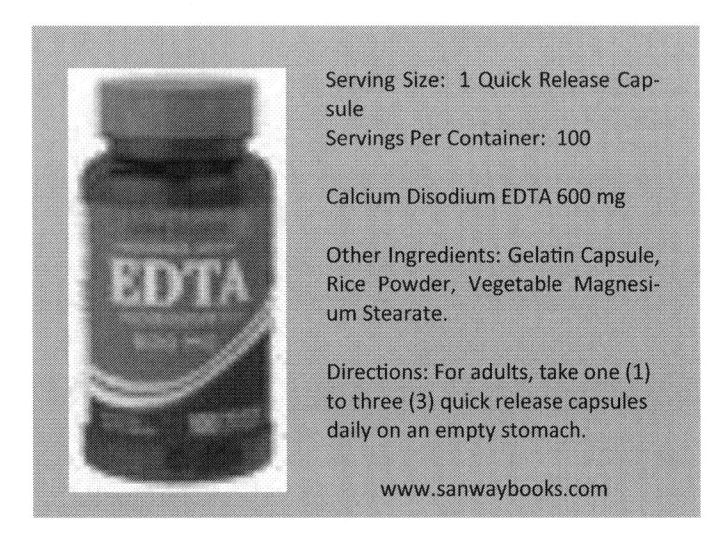

Serving Size: 1 Quick Release Capsule
Servings Per Container: 100

Calcium Disodium EDTA 600 mg

Other Ingredients: Gelatin Capsule, Rice Powder, Vegetable Magnesium Stearate.

Directions: For adults, take one (1) to three (3) quick release capsules daily on an empty stomach.

www.sanwaybooks.com

What it Means to be a Member of Silent Angels Network

Silent Angels Nonprofit was established in 1991, for the purpose helping homeless and disaster victims. Blankets were distributed by the thousands. One memorable trip was to Washington, DC. We carried three pick up trucks, two trailers and two cars, all loaded with blankets, clothes and food.

Silent Angels soon grew to where the members were helping various needs coast to coast in the USA, and several foreign countries. Everyone who volunteered through the years, counted it a blessing to serve.

In recent months, Silent Angels became a Network, which would allow its members to do a greater service in helping others. The Membership Plan was successful from the start. We have members from America, Kenya, Cameroon, Nigeria, Uganda, India, The Netherlands, and Pakistan.

Why the Excitement?

Members of Silent Angels Network are excited for several reasons.

- Membership helps to support missionaries in foreign fields to teach the Great Commission, that Jesus gave in Matthew 28:19-20.
- Memberships help to feed the hunger in underprivileged countries.
- Memberships help to provide medications for the sick.
- Memberships help to provide an income to local mission workers, so they can preach, teach and otherwise serve God without working farms and other jobs.
- Membership helps you to be a part of the great commission without leaving your country.

A Few Accomplishments of Silent Angels Network

- Blankets for homeless and disaster victims
- Delivered blankets to the west coast where homeless in so bad.
- Provided household furnishings to victims of a fire & others.
- Provided medicine and other health needs.
- Donated medical supplies to St. Luke's Free Hospital.
- Bought firefighter's equipment.
- Provided funds for Asian storm victims.
- Assisted Gospel Partners (mission work in India)
- Assisted Southeastern Children's Home.
- Organized "Youth Motivation" a mission (Uganda).
- Assisted with the rebuilding of New Orleans in 2006.
- Delivered a truck and a trailer load of medical needs to Mississippi after Katrina hit the southern coast.
- Provided bottled water after hurricanes and tornados.
- Built an orphan's home in Zambia, 2009.

(Continued next page)

Silent Angels Network Magazine

Other Reasons Why Members are Excited

Members are also excited because they can earn an income while helping others. We are using this plan to reach more people faster.

When a member enrolls another member, they earn a commission. (See the chart on Membership page.)

Fee: This is the fee that the new member pays for their membership.

Mission: This is the amount that the mission receives from the new member.

Sponsor: This is the amount the sponsor earns for enrolling the new member.

Expense: Company expenses.

Bonuses: The amount that is placed in the bonus account and shared by members.

The Bonus Plan

Perhaps the bonus plan is one of the most exciting part of the pay plan. We work together in a co-op (Working together for the good of all).

This principle is taught in the Bible. "We who are strong ought to bear with the failings of the weak and not to please ourselves." Romans 15:1.

Also "Two are better than one, because they have a good return for their labor: If either of them falls down, one can help the other up. But pity anyone who falls and has no one to help them up. Also, if two lie down together, they will keep warm. But how can one keep warm alone? Though one may be overpowered, two can defend themselves. A cord of three strands is not quickly broken." Ecclesiastes 4:9-12

For these reasons, all bonuses go into a special account. When a member's account has accumulated $32.00 we send them a check. This avoids writing so many small checks. A member may qualify for multiple checks.

How Bonuses Are Earned

You Earn Bonuses When You ...
- Enroll as a member of as a member of Silent Angels Network.
- When you enroll a new member.
- When you place an ad in this magazine.
- When you purchase healthcare products in the General Store.
- When you purchase from the Book Store.
- When you purchase Children's books.
- When you publish a book.

Go online to www.sanwaybooks.com. Click on "Membership" in the menu to join as a member of Silent Angels Network.

The sooner you enroll, the sooner you will start getting checks.

Start telling your friends about the Silent Angels Network Memberships

Made in the USA
Columbia, SC
09 July 2021